Best Easy Day Hikes
Des Moines

Help Us Keep This Guide Up to Date

Every effort has been made by the author and editors to make this guide as accurate and useful as possible. However, many things can change after a guide is published—trails are rerouted, regulations change, facilities come under new management, etc.

We would appreciate hearing from you concerning your experiences with this guide and how you feel it could be improved and kept up to date. While we may not be able to respond to all comments and suggestions, we'll take them to heart and we'll also make certain to share them with the author. Please send your comments and suggestions to the following address:

GPP
Reader Response/Editorial Department
P.O. Box 480
Guilford, CT 06437

Or you may e-mail us at:

editorial@GlobePequot.com

Thanks for your input, and happy trails!

Best Easy Day Hikes Series

Best Easy Day Hikes Des Moines

Michael Ream

FALCONGUIDES

GUILFORD, CONNECTICUT
HELENA, MONTANA

AN IMPRINT OF GLOBE PEQUOT PRESS

To buy books in quantity for corporate use
or incentives, call **(800) 962–0973**
or e-mail **premiums@GlobePequot.com**.

FALCONGUIDES®

Copyright © 2011 by Morris Book Publishing, LLC

FalconGuides is an imprint of Globe Pequot Press.
Falcon, FalconGuides, and Outfit Your Mind are registered trademarks
of Morris Book Publishing, LLC.

Layout: Kevin Mak
Project editor: Gregory Hyman
Maps by Mapping Specialists Ltd. © Morris Book Publishing, LLC

TOPO! Explorer software and SuperQuad source maps courtesy of
National Geographic Maps. For information about TOPO! Explorer,
TOPO!, and Nat Geo Maps products, go to www.topo.com or www
.natgeomaps.com.

Library of Congress Cataloging-in-Publication data is available on file.

ISBN 978-0-7627-6991-9

Printed in the United States of America

10 9 8 7 6 5 4 3 2 1

Contents

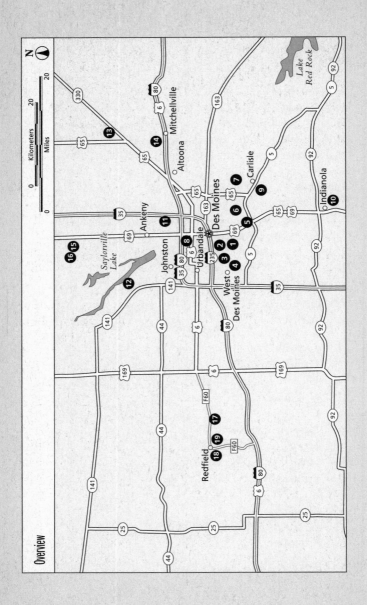

Overview

Acknowledgments

Thanks are due to the helpful people at county conservation boards and parks and recreation departments in Des
Moines and surrounding communities, as well as at the Iowa
Natural Heritage Foundation, who provided me with maps
and information on the numerous hiking opportunities in
central Iowa. I am indebted to all of them for their extensive
knowledge of local trails. Their help has made the hikes in
this guide that much more interesting and informative.

Local outdoor enthusiasts whom I met along the way
were also an invaluable source of tips and advice on trails
and hiking. Keep up the hiking spirit—there are always
more trails to discover!

Finally, thanks to all at Globe Pequot Press, especially
Jessica Haberman and project editor Gregory Hyman,
whose advice and insight helped make this project possible.

Introduction

Surrounded by seemingly endless cornfields stretching across the flat countryside to the horizon, Des Moines might seem like an unlikely choice for great hiking. Yet there are plenty of interesting trails and hiking treasures hidden in the vast sweep of farmland that defines central Iowa. Numerous trail-filled parks dot the region, offering hikers everything from majestic views overlooking a scenic river valley to excellent wildflower viewing opportunities to tours of restored wetlands, which provide an ideal habitat for a wide variety of wildlife.

A number of rivers and creeks, often meandering through wooded areas, bisect the landscape and help to break up the views of long rows of corn and soybeans. Miles upon miles of cycling paths are also well used by hikers, and are a good choice for easy hikes due to their long, flat stretches.

Des Moines, by far the largest city in Iowa, with a population of roughly 200,000 in the city proper and close to a half million in its metropolitan area, has undergone a renaissance of sorts in recent years, and now boasts a revitalized downtown with busy office buildings, a new library, and numerous restaurants and nightlife options. At the junction of the Des Moines and Raccoon Rivers stands Principal Park, home to the minor-league affiliate of the Chicago Cubs, which is often packed on game days.

Standing tall on a hill overlooking downtown is the gold dome of the Iowa State Capitol. West of downtown is the campus of Drake University, home to some 5,000 students, while farther west is the booming suburb of West Des Moines, with corporate campuses and residential subdivisions marching into the cornfields. Outside a handful of villages transformed into bedroom communities for Des Moines, small towns in the countryside still have a pastoral, Norman Rockwellish feel, with charming farmhouses, barns and town squares, and windmills, silos, and grain elevators dominating the skylines.

Des Moines has an impressive number of trails, used mainly by cyclists but patronized by hikers as well, which weave through the city and suburbs and run into the countryside, where several trails link together to run for many miles. Eighteen nature and wilderness parks and trails are sprinkled around Des Moines and in surrounding Polk County, preserving some 12,000 acres of woodlands, prairies, and wetlands, and offering excellent opportunities for cycling, camping, and other activities, in addition to hiking. Nearby Dallas and Warren Counties are stocked with extensive parks and trails as well.

Weather

Because Des Moines is located in the heart of the Midwest and has a topography with virtually no natural features to buffer weather fronts that sweep across its flat surfaces, hikers may find themselves at the mercy of extreme weather. There are definitely four distinct seasons here, with temperatures that can range from over 100 degrees F in the summer months to well below zero in the winter. Some trails and parks may shut down as a result of inclement weather, so it's always a good idea to check out conditions and possible closures before you set out on a hike.

Spring and fall are often very pleasant, with wildflowers blooming in the spring and leaves changing color in the fall.

During the summer you will want to bring a hat, sunscreen, and plenty of water on your hikes to deal with the blazing sunshine.

Winter brings snow and a lot of it: Drifts can pile up several feet in a single snowstorm, blocking trails and creating icy, hazardous conditions on roads. Open fields provide little surface friction to stop winds that whip across the state, thus leading to the spectacular blizzards of prairie legend, with blowing snow causing "whiteout" conditions that severely diminish vision and make it impossible to drive. Wind is a feature of the weather in central Iowa for much of the year, especially in rural areas, where it comes gusting off surrounding farm fields. Though it's often not that unpleasant, it can still be an unwelcome surprise. Tornado season runs from roughly April through October—keep abreast of tornado watches and warnings during these months. If you see a greenish glow in the sky, get to shelter immediately, preferably in a basement. Tornado winds can gust up to 500 miles per hour and can appear with almost no warning.

In summer, precipitation comes in the form of rain, with the occasional thunderstorm. Keep an eye out for gathering storm clouds and get to shelter if you see them rolling in—lightning is the most immediate danger, but storms can also lead to flash floods from creeks. Violent hailstorms are also a possibility—you do not want to get caught in one of these, so pay attention to warnings. Excessive rainfall can flood trails very quickly. Be aware of rain forecasts, especially if you are hiking near creeks or rivers, and call to see about trail conditions if you are heading out soon after a heavy rainstorm.

Trail Regulations

The hikes in this book are on trails maintained by different county conservation boards and city park departments. Trail regulations thus vary, so take note of the details in each trail listing. Most of the urban trails and many rural trails are free, but some do charge to hike on them. Some trails require fees or accept donations in order to assist with maintenance—those that do are noted in the hike listings.

Dogs are permitted on some trails, but not others. Some trails allow only hikers while others are multiuse, permitting cyclists, horseback riders, and other users. Some trails close at different times of the year, including unforeseen closings due to weather or other issues. Thus, it's always a good idea to contact trail managers to see if there is anything you need to know. You can also get an idea if a trail is going to be heavily used on the day you plan to hike—nothing is worse than planning for a wilderness hiking getaway, arriving at the trail, and discovering it overrun with large, noisy school groups.

Supervising agencies and their websites are a good source for maps and information on trails, including trail closures. Most trails in this book are easily accessible, although a few are located down winding country roads, not always with signs pointing the way—be sure to check directions before you set out on the more remote hikes. Some of the more rural hikes are in areas open for hunting, which begins in late summer and runs through the fall and into winter—it's worth seeing if this applies before you head out to the trail.

Safety and Preparation

Hiking is a great way to see a bit of nature, get some exercise, and in general have a pleasant day in the great outdoors.

However, before you hit the trail, it's a good idea to take the time to make sure you are prepared for your hike. Just a little preparation can mean the difference between a good hike and one that turns into a hassle—or worse.

The biggest hazards when hiking in central Iowa are sunburn, ticks and mosquitoes, and poison ivy, which grows along many of the trails listed in this guide. Take time to put on sunscreen and bug repellent. Learn to identify poison ivy so you can spot it on the trail: "Leaves of three, let it be." Poison ivy is also a good reason not to veer off the trail and into the woods. Tick bites can be painful as well as transmit diseases—check yourself for ticks after a hike and learn how to remove the little critters, as well as identify the symptoms of Lyme disease and other ailments carried by some ticks.

Good hiking shoes are a must on wilderness trails, and are recommended for urban trails as well. It's also not a bad idea to invest in some decent hiking socks. There are different kinds, so use the best for the weather—lightweight socks for summer, wool or heavy synthetic socks for cooler days. Choose comfortable clothing appropriate for the season—loose-fitting, "breathable" clothes for summer, warmer clothes for winter. Synthetic fabrics generally provide much better protection in wet weather than cotton. In addition, you'll want a wide-brimmed hat for summer and a warm hat for winter: The sun can fry your head in minutes, and much of the body's heat escapes through an uncovered head. Sunglasses help on bright and sunny days.

Put together a small backpack of hiking essentials. You may not use all of this stuff, especially if you're not hiking in a wilderness area, but it's worth having just in case.

- **Water.** Really, this is the most important item. Dehydration is a greater risk when hiking than many people realize. Symptoms include fatigue, headache, and general confusion. Bring plenty of water and drink some regularly. Ideally, carry two or more bottles, so that if you lose one you still have some water. Fill up your water bottles before you start your hike—many trailheads do not have water sources. The water in many streams and creeks is not safe for drinking.

- **Food.** Carry at least some snack items (not junk food!), such as granola bars or trail mix. Sometimes a hike takes much longer than you anticipated and it's good to have some food for energy.

- **Trail map.** An absolute necessity. Many trails are not well marked, and there are often "unofficial" trails that connect with the trail you are on. These will only get you lost if you take them. It's also not a bad idea to learn how to use a compass with a map.

- **Clothes.** Bring extra clothes in case the ones you have on get too wet to wear. Don't go overboard—usually an extra shirt and a pair of socks is sufficient. **Rain gear** is another good item to have, particularly during the rainy season or if even a slight chance of rain is forecast. Carry a rain jacket or pullover and some rain pants you can pull over your hiking pants. You can also get a rain cover for your pack if it's not waterproof.

- **Cell phone.** Carrying a phone is becoming more common on trails these days, but remember that service is often not available in remote, rural areas. Use it only for genuine emergencies, and please, please put it on vibrate. Remember, you came hiking to be in a peaceful, natural setting, without annoying cell phone rings!

- **Bug repellent and sunscreen.** These prevent a lot of aggravation. Use them.

- **Watch.** You don't want to get stuck in a rural state park after it closes for the evening and they shut the gate, do you?

- And of course, **this book.**

To make yourself the complete hiker, consider bringing the following as well. These items are not really necessities, but you may find a use for them:

- GPS
- Camera
- Pocketknife
- Walking stick
- Binoculars
- Field guides
- Journal and pen

Leave No Trace

Trails are heavily used during the warmer months. We, as trail users and advocates, must be especially vigilant to make sure our passage leaves no lasting mark. Here are some basic guidelines for preserving trails in the region:

- Pack out all your own trash, including biodegradable items like orange peels. You might also pack out garbage left by less-considerate hikers.

- Avoid damaging trailside soils and plants by remaining on the established route. Social trails created by hikers, cyclists, and off-road vehicles are a plague on area parklands, contributing to erosion problems and creating unsightly scars on the landscape. Don't cut switchbacks, which can promote erosion.

- Don't approach or feed any wild creatures—the squirrel eyeing your snack food is best able to survive if it remains self-reliant.

- Don't pick wildflowers or gather rocks, antlers, feathers, and other treasures along the trail. Removing these items will only take away from the next hiker's experience.

- Be courteous by not making loud noises while hiking.

- Many of these trails are multiuse, which means you'll share them with other hikers, trail runners, mountain bikers, and equestrians. Familiarize yourself with the proper trail etiquette, yielding the trail when appropriate.

- Use outhouses at trailheads or along the trail.

How to Use This Guide

This guide is designed to be simple and easy to use. Each hike is described with a map and summary information that delivers the trail's vital statistics including length, difficulty, fees and permits, park hours, canine compatibility, and trail contacts. Directions to the trailhead are also provided, along with a general description of what you'll see along the way. A detailed route finder (Miles and Directions) sets forth mileages between significant landmarks along the trail.

How the Hikes Were Chosen

This guide describes trails that are accessible to every hiker, whether visiting from out of town or a local resident. The hikes are no longer than 11 miles round-trip, and most are considerably shorter. They range in difficulty from flat excursions perfect for a family outing to more challenging treks with moderate climbs. I've selected hikes in the heart of Des Moines, in nearby suburban areas, and in rural areas that require a trip down winding country roads to reach the trailhead. While these trails are among the best, keep in mind that nearby trails, sometimes in the same park or sometimes in a neighboring open space, may offer options better suited to your needs.

Selecting a Hike

These are all easy hikes, but easy is a relative term. Hike difficulty is determined this way:

- **Easy** hikes are generally short and flat, taking no longer than an hour to complete.

- **Moderate** hikes involve increased distance and relatively mild changes in elevation, and will take one to two hours to complete.
- **More challenging** hikes feature some steep stretches, greater distances, and generally take longer than two hours to complete.

Keep in mind that what you think is easy is entirely dependent on your level of fitness and the adequacy of your gear (primarily shoes). Use the trail's length as a gauge of its relative difficulty—even if climbing is involved it won't be bad if the hike is less than 1 mile long. If you are hiking with a group, select a hike that's appropriate for the least fit and prepared in your party.

Approximate hiking times are based on the assumption that on flat ground, most walkers average 2 miles per hour. Adjust that rate by the steepness of the terrain and your level of fitness (subtract time if you're an aerobic animal and add time if you're hiking with kids), and you have a ballpark hiking duration. Be sure to add more time if you plan to picnic or take part in other activities like bird watching or photography.

Trail Finder

Best Hikes for Children

Best Hikes for Great Views, Vistas, and Skylines

Best Hikes for Nature Lovers

Best Fast Hikes for Rural Landscapes

Map Legend

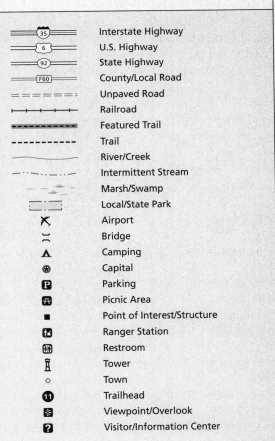

	Interstate Highway
	U.S. Highway
	State Highway
	County/Local Road
	Unpaved Road
	Railroad
	Featured Trail
	Trail
	River/Creek
	Intermittent Stream
	Marsh/Swamp
	Local/State Park
	Airport
	Bridge
	Camping
	Capital
	Parking
	Picnic Area
	Point of Interest/Structure
	Ranger Station
	Restroom
	Tower
	Town
	Trailhead
	Viewpoint/Overlook
	Visitor/Information Center

1   Great Western Trail

Beginning on the edge of Water Works Park, a large open green space south of downtown Des Moines, this trail on a former railroad bed winds past the outer edge of Des Moines International Airport yet maintains a wilderness feel, with thick foliage and the occasional deer sighting. It is very popular with cyclists, who zip out of the city and into open country, stopping every few miles at small-town taverns that serve as popular watering holes. (In fact, this hike is perhaps best done in the middle of the day or early afternoon, before the path becomes crowded with cyclists.)

Distance: 11.0 miles out and back

Approximate hiking time: 5 to 6 hours

Difficulty: More challenging due to hike length

Trail surface: Paved path

Best seasons: Spring through fall

Other trail users: Cyclists, cross-country skiers

Canine compatibility: Leashed dogs permitted

Fees and permits: None

Schedule: Sunrise to sunset daily

Maps: USGS Des Moines SW; trail map available from contact listed below

Trail contact: Polk County Conservation, 11407 NW Jester Park Dr., Granger 50109; (515) 323-5300; www.leadingyououtdoors.org. (Trail is jointly managed with Warren County Conservation.)

Other: No horses allowed; water and restrooms available in Water Works Park, near the trailhead

Finding the trailhead: From I-235, take exit 4 (IA 28/63rd Street) and head south on IA 28. Drive south 2.7 miles to Park Avenue and turn left, heading east. Drive 1.3 miles to Valley Drive/ George Flagg Parkway, where you turn left and then right into a small parking area located across the street from the Izaak Walton League building. The trail runs in front of the parking area—as you are facing the path, turn right and follow it toward Park Avenue. GPS: N41 33.312' / W93 40.753'

The Hike

A block from the start of the hike, you reach Park Avenue. Cross the street and resume walking on the trail—it's the paved path on your right. (You'll probably pass a number of vehicles with bike racks parked alongside the path, belonging to cyclists who are out on the trail.) Moving into a wooded area, walk past a wide swath of Queen Anne's lace. Overgrown trees and bushes alongside the path make for good baffles against noise from nearby roads.

Shortly after heading into the woods, listen for the roar of jet engines—you may see an airliner swoop in a few hundred feet overhead as it takes off or lands on the runways of Des Moines International Airport to your left, just past the airport fences hidden behind the cluster of trees. Black-eyed Susans and purple coneflowers are among the flora that blooms along this trail, as are numerous cattails in a marshy area on your left as you move past the edge of the airport.

After winding around a few curves, the path unkinks for a long, straight stretch, with the rolling green berms of the airport still on your left, while the wooded area on your right is thick with greenery. Deer are not as prevalent on this hike as they are on other local trails, but you still may spot one or two bounding through the trees on the right side of the path.

Continuing through marshlike bottomlands, the trail intersects SW McKinley Avenue at the corner of the airport. Moving along the path into the countryside, you pass

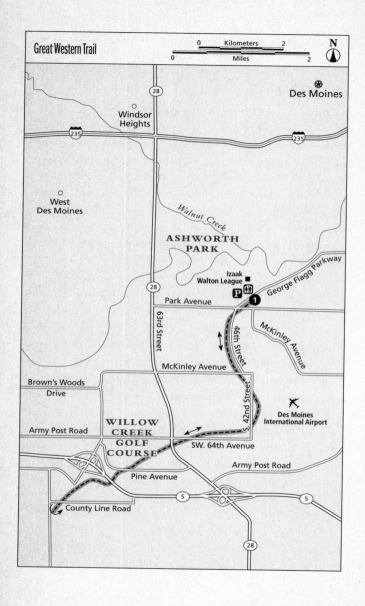

Great Western Trail

Kilometers 0 — 2
Miles 0 — 2

N

Des Moines

28

Windsor
Heights

235   235

West
Des Moines

Walnut Creek

ASHWORTH
PARK

Izaak
Walton League

P   George Flagg Parkway

28   Park Avenue   1

63rd Street   46th Street   McKinley Avenue

McKinley Avenue

Brown's Woods
Drive   S. 42nd Street

Des Moines
International Airport

WILLOW
CREEK
GOLF
COURSE

Army Post Road   SW. 64th Avenue

Army Post Road

Pine Avenue

5   5

County Line Road

28

scrubby cottonwoods as Frink Creek winds lazily to your right, with frogs occasionally hopping across in front of you.

As you cross 42nd Street then loop around and cross it again, the path veers west-southwest and the creek is now on your left. The scenery opens up here, with a meadow on your left and a farm field on the right. The echo of jet engines still resounds through the sky, but you can also catch sight of deer roaming through the meadow.

A stretch through Willow Creek Golf Course gives you the opportunity for a water break—just be alert for carts zipping across the path! After leaving the golf course, you soon come to a marshy area with cattails. Farther on, a path-side bench is a good place to stop and rest a bit. Then you reach Bambino's restaurant, where you can fuel up on some Italian grub before heading back to the trailhead.

Miles and Directions

0.0   Start by heading away from the Izaak Walton League building and crossing Park Avenue. Follow the path as it runs parallel to SW 46th Street.

0.6   Tree cover opens up slightly on your left, giving you a look at the fences on the edge of the airport.

0.9   Follow the path as it extends out for a long, straight stretch.

1.2   Reach the intersection of the path with SW McKinley Avenue, at SW 46th Street.

1.6   Cross 42nd Street and continue on the path.

3.3   After passing under the overpass for Army Post Road/SW 64th Avenue, walk through the tunnel under 60th Street. Continue on the path as it moves past a gate and through Willow Creek Golf Course. (Water and portable toilets are available here.)

4.2 Follow the path as it passes the intersection of Pine Avenue and South Eighth Street on the left. Continue on the path as it moves toward the tunnel under IA 5.

5.5 After crossing County Line Road, reach South Orilla Road and Bambino's restaurant. Turn around and head back toward the trailhead.

11.0 Arrive back at the trailhead.

2 Walnut Creek Trail

A lowland trail that eventually hooks onto both the Great Western and Clive Greenbelt Trails, this hike takes you through the woods and past a languid stretch of Walnut Creek, dotted with small islands where deer and other wildlife occasionally swim and rest. Like other trails in and around Des Moines, this one is popular with cyclists and can get slightly crowded on weekends and in the early evenings. *Note:* The trail is not well marked, so pay careful attention to the hike directions.

Distance: 9.4 miles out and back
Approximate hiking time: 4 to 5 hours
Difficulty: More challenging due to hike length
Trail surface: Paved path
Best seasons: Spring through fall
Other trail users: Cyclists
Canine compatibility: Leashed dogs permitted
Fees and permits: None
Schedule: Sunrise to sunset daily
Maps: USGS Des Moines SW; trail map available from contacts listed below
Trail contacts: Des Moines Parks and Recreation, 600 East Court Ave., Des Moines 50309; (515) 237-1386; www.dmparks .org. Clive Parks & Recreation, 1900 NW 114th St., Clive 50325; (515) 223-5246; www .cityofclive.com/departments/ parks-recreation/
Special considerations: Flooding of this trail is a real possibility after heavy rains. Check with the parks department to see if the trail has been closed.

Finding the trailhead: Exit I-235 at 42nd Street and head south. Drive 0.5 mile to Grand Avenue and turn right, heading west. Drive 3 blocks to 45th Street and turn left just before the Des Moines Art

Center into Greenwood/Ashworth Park. Drive 0.5 mile, passing an amphitheater and pond on your right, then Ashworth Pool on your left. Park just past the swimming pool, where the path runs into the woods next to some benches and a bike rack. GPS: N41 34.562' / W93 40.998'

The Hike

Heading away from the swimming pool, climb a small rise in the trail and then cross railroad tracks. After turning right at a path junction, walk with Walnut Creek on your left, alongside low-lying, swampy areas full of chirping birds. Take a moment and listen to the different calls ringing through the air.

A wide spot on the left side of the path opens up, and you may catch sight of a heron skimming over the creek waters. (After rainstorms, the banks along the path here will be slick with mud and standing water, which often floods onto the path itself.) Walnut Creek contains more than twenty species of fish, including sunfish, bluegill, and carp. The woods are home to animals such as raccoon, beaver, and deer.

Pass an open green field on your left, home to a variety of birds, and then a large, sandy island in the middle of the creek. On your right, the path runs past the backyards of a residential neighborhood.

Continuing along the path, you will see numerous feeder streams flowing through the swampy lowlands and into the creek, as well as the railroad tracks visible on your right through the thick stands of trees.

The path opens up a bit and then reaches an intersection with North Valley Drive, next to a bridge crossing the creek. Take time to look out at the creek waters, which rush over a small dam and waterfall just beyond the bridge.

The creek widens on the left as the path gradually moves above it. You pass a complex of soccer fields on the right as you approach the Grand Avenue overpass, just east of 63rd Street and the old commercial district of Valley Junction.

Crossing railroad tracks, follow the path as it loops left and very briefly parallels 62nd Street before heading back into a wooded area with Walnut Creek on your left again. Crossing two bridges over channels that flow into the creek, you also pass a spur trail running to the right—stay on the main path. There are lots of birds here, ranging from robins and cardinals flitting through the trees to geese flying overhead.

The creek really opens up on this stretch, with sandbars poking up in shallow spots. After passing a dog run on your right, you reach Colby Park, which has water and restrooms. Soon after, the Walnut Creek Trail splits off to the north, running through a residential neighborhood. Stay on the path along the creek, which becomes the Clive Greenbelt Trail after you cross under the 73rd Street overpass.

Continuing along the creek, you'll see some small waterfalls beneath an old railroad bridge. Crossing the tracks, you'll soon spot some squat, white oil tanks to your right and then arrive in Greenbelt Park just after the 86th Street overpass.

This is the turnaround spot; return as you came. Note: This is also the starting point for the Clive Greenbelt Trail hike, if you're interested in a full-day excursion. (There are fast-food restaurants on nearby 86th Street if you need a pit stop.)

Walnut Creek Trail

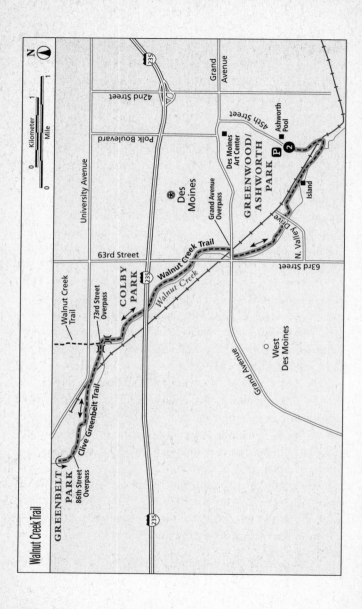

Miles and Directions

0.0 Start by walking down the path away from the swimming pool.

0.4 Cross the railroad tracks and come to a T junction. Take the right fork and continue to follow the path.

0.9 Walk past a large island sitting in the middle of the creek on your left.

1.3 Reach the intersection with North Valley Drive. Cross the street and continue on the path.

1.9 Walk under the Grand Avenue overpass, just east of 63rd Street.

3.1 Reach Colby Park. Follow the path as it winds around a Wal-Mart parking lot.

3.6 Follow the path as it veers left, runs under the 73rd Street overpass, and becomes the Clive Greenbelt Trail.

4.7 After crossing Walnut Creek on a bridge, follow the path under the 86th Street overpass, cross another bridge over Walnut Creek, and arrive in Greenbelt Park. Turn around here and return to the trailhead.

9.4 Arrive back at the trailhead.

3 Clive Greenbelt Trail

This trail forms a bridge between the Walnut Creek Trail and the eastern edge of the Raccoon River Valley Trail as it heads into the countryside west of Des Moines. Beginning just off a busy road that straddles the suburbs of Clive, Windsor Heights, and West Des Moines, the hike meanders along a bucolic stretch of Walnut Creek, making for an easy escape from the surrounding bustle (although the path can become crowded with cyclists—stay alert!). The hike features a reconstructed prairie alive with flora—it's probably the best example of prairie you'll see on any hike in this guide.

Distance: 7.0 miles out and back
Approximate hiking time: 3.5 hours
Difficulty: More challenging due to hike length
Trail surface: Paved path
Best seasons: Spring through fall
Other trail users: Cyclists
Canine compatibility: Leashed dogs permitted
Fees and permits: None
Schedule: 5:30 a.m. to 10:30 p.m. daily
Maps: USGS Des Moines SW; USGS Commerce. Trail map

available from Clive and Des Moines Parks and Recreation departments.
Trail contact: Clive Parks & Recreation, 1900 NW 114th St., Clive 50325; (515) 223-5246; www.cityofclive.com/departments/parks-recreation/
Special considerations: The trail is subject to flooding from the creek, especially after heavy rains. Check with trail managers to make sure the trail is open before heading out.
Other: Water fountains located at intervals along the trail

Finding the trailhead: From I-235, take exit 2 (22nd Street), heading north. Drive 0.7 mile, crossing University Avenue and entering Clive, where the road becomes 86th Street/Clive Road. Cross the bridge over Walnut Creek and immediately turn left onto a small, unmarked street next to a car repair shop and oil change outlet, and across the street from a complex of oil tanks. Park in the lot for Greenbelt Park, next to the path. GPS: N41 36.226' / W93 44.279'

The Hike

The hike begins with a transition away from the urbanized congestion of strip malls and auto shops and into the woodlands along the creek. Soon a wide bend of the creek opens up on your left and the trail plunges into deeper woods. Crickets chirp, and birds hop in the trees.

Keep your eyes on the creek—you may see a flock of geese or a lone heron zoom overhead. The greenbelt, which covers 180 acres of protected forest, is also home to redheaded woodpeckers, opossums, and white-tailed deer.

Railroad tracks poke through the trees on your right as you move along the path, and a waterfall spills over a culvert. The creek picks up speed a bit, flowing past downed trees and curving around sandy banks. The still-thick growth of trees features numerous oaks, with branches bending so densely above the path that in some places they blot out the sky. Other trees in the greenbelt include walnut, cottonwood, and box elder.

After moving farther down the path, you find yourself walking atop low bluffs perched over the creek. As you reach 100th Street, look off to your left, where a small waterfall spills over and into the creek.

After walking under the 100th Street overpass, cross another bridge, then come to the reconstructed prairie on

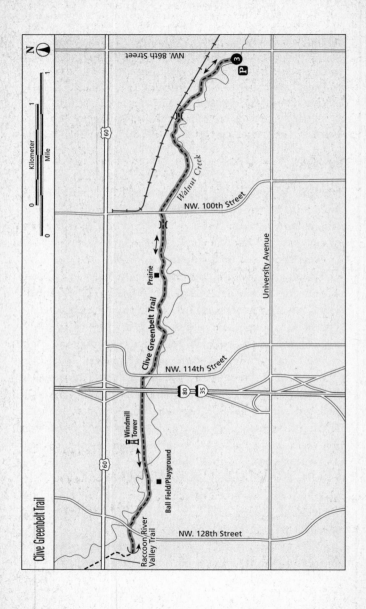

Clive Greenbelt Trail

N

NW. 86th Street

Walnut Creek

Clive Greenbelt Trail

Prairie

NW. 100th Street

NW. 114th Street

University Avenue

Windmill
Tower

Ball Field/Playground

Raccoon/River
Valley Trail

NW. 128th Street

Kilometer

Mile

your right. Thirty species of native grasses were planted to create this prairie, similar to those that once covered 80 percent of Iowa. Today there are less than 4,000 acres of virgin prairie left in the state.

Walking past the prairie, pass a spur trail on the left—stay on the main path. There are two more spur paths, with the second one leading to 108th Street and Lincoln Avenue—again, stay on the main path. The hum of traffic grows louder as you approach the 114th Street overpass, where a side path leads to Clive's public library and swimming pool. Soon after, you cross under I-80/35. Note the water gauge on the concrete pylon; flooding sometimes occurs here.

Keep your eyes peeled for an old windmill tower on the right, with vines growing up it. You then cross a bridge over Walnut Creek at a spot with a beautiful series of small waterfalls. The creek is on your right after the crossing.

A ball field and playground ringed by some impressive willow trees and oak saplings on your left signal you are nearing the junction with the Raccoon River Valley Trail, which splits off to the right. The Clive Greenbelt Trail continues on to the left, but this is a good spot to head back to the trailhead.

Miles and Directions

0.0   Start by walking down the path by the trail information signboard, with the creek on your left.

0.5   Follow the path as it curves alongside railroad tracks on your right. Shortly after, come to a fork in the trail, with the right-hand path leading to Swanson Boulevard. Take the left-hand path and cross a bridge over a stream that feeds the creek.

0.7 Walk past a bridge on your left, marked NW 93rd Court and Lincoln Avenue, and continue walking on the path.

1.1 Walk past a smaller path that forks off to your right. Continue on the main path and cross a bridge. Just past the bridge is an overpass for 100th Street. Continue walking straight, passing under 100th Street.

1.6 Pass a playground on your right, then reach the reconstructed prairie on your right. A sign explains the history and plant life of the prairie.

2.3 Walk under the NW 114th Street overpass. Follow the path as it veers left, and walk under the I-80/35 overpass.

2.7 Pass a spur trail on the left and an access driveway on the right. Continue on the main path.

3.3 Pass a ball field and playground on the left and walk under the NW 128th Street overpass.

3.5 Reach an intersection with the Raccoon River Valley Trail. Turn around and retrace your route to Greenbelt Park and the trailhead.

7.0 Arrive back at the trailhead.

4 Brown's Woods Nature Trail

This hike is a "double loop," or two trails linked together, and is located inside the largest urban forest preserve in Iowa: Brown's Woods, 484 wooded acres that hug the Raccoon River just inside the Des Moines suburb of West Des Moines. Brown's Woods is also part of the Makoke (MAH-koh-kay) birding trail, which encompasses several sites in central Iowa. The hike is notable for the cacophonous sound of woodpeckers at work, including the yellow-bellied sapsucker and yellow-brown flicker.

Distance: 1.9-mile double loop
Approximate hiking time: 1 hour
Difficulty: Moderate due to several hills, and the trail can get muddy
Trail surface: Dirt
Best seasons: Spring through fall
Other trail users: Cross-country skiers
Canine compatibility: Leashed dogs permitted
Fees and permits: None
Schedule: 8 a.m. to sunset daily

Maps: USGS Des Moines SW; trail map posted at parking area
Trail contact: Polk County Conservation, 11407 NW Jester Park Dr., Granger 50109; (515) 323-5300; www.leadingyououtdoors .org
Special considerations: Prone to flooding after heavy rains. Check with the trail manager to see if the trail has been closed.
Other: Cyclists and horses prohibited due to trails' sensitivity to erosion; small portable toilet at trailhead, but no water

Finding the trailhead: Follow I-235 to exit 4 (IA 28/63rd Street) and head south on IA 28. Drive 3.7 miles to Brown's Woods Drive and turn right, then drive 0.3 mile to the parking area on your right. Alternate route: Take I-35 to exit 68 (IA 5) and head east on IA 5.

Drive 5 miles and take exit 99 (IA 28), heading north. Drive 2.2 miles on IA 28 to Brown's Woods Drive and turn left. Drive 0.3 mile to the parking area on your right. GPS: N41 32.496' / W93 42.522'

The Hike

The noise of jets climbing into the air from the nearby Des Moines International Airport is a fairly regular sound on this hike, but it fades away as you head out on the Preparation Loop, the first half of the hike, and find yourself in a heavily wooded forest. Lush vegetation lines both sides of the trail, and moss grows up the sides of tree trunks. Keep an eye out for poison ivy, which isn't always easy to see in the dense, shaded plant cover along the path.

After picking up the Wilderness Loop for the second part of the hike, stop for a moment and listen for the sound of rushing water—you are close to a creek that flows near the trail. As you descend the hill, look to your right to try and catch a glimpse of a small waterfall.

Moving along the path, you may see white-tailed deer bounding through the thick woods and hopping over downed limbs, although the main animal activity remains the tapping of woodpeckers on tree trunks. Blue violets are among the smattering of woodland wildflowers you may spot alongside the path.

After returning to the trail junction that links the two loops, resume walking on the Preparation Loop for the last part of the hike. Swing close to the creek again before coming within range of the sound of traffic and ending the hike. The open sky at the trailhead is a nice change from the dark, shaded paths, with sunlight largely blocked out by the majestic trees.

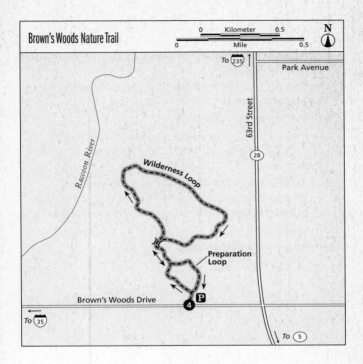

Brown's Woods Nature Trail

0 — Kilometer — 0.5
0 — Mile — 0.5

N

To 235↑
Park Avenue

Raccoon River

Wilderness Loop

63rd Street

28

Preparation
Loop

Brown's Woods Drive

To 35 ←

4 P

To 5

Miles and Directions

0.0 Begin by walking a short distance into the woods, then reach a junction and take the left fork. Follow the path as it curves to the right (in a clockwise direction).

0.2 The path begins a descent of a gentle slope. After the descent, reach a junction and take the left fork—you are now on the Wilderness Loop. Descend another slope and continue on the path.

0.3 Reach a bridge that spans a creek. Cross to the other side and begin walking up a slope. Reach a fork in the trail and veer left, staying on the main path.

0.7 Descend a steeper slope. At the bottom of the slope, continue walking along the path as it ascends another hill, passing a path that forks off to the left along the way. (Stay on the main path.)

0.9 Continue walking straight along the main path, passing a smaller trail that forks off to the left.

1.2 The path narrows, then widens.

1.5 Reach a T junction—you have completed the Wilderness Loop. Turn left, walking back on the Preparation Loop toward the trailhead.

1.6 Reach another T junction. Turn left and continue back toward the trailhead, walking with a creek on your left. Pass a smaller trail on your left as you move back toward the trailhead.

1.9 Arrive back at the trailhead.

5 Fort Des Moines Park Nature Trail

With scenery including both a large pond and stands of aspen and oak trees, this hike at a park built on the site of a former cavalry post is a fairly easy walk alongside water and through woods. The park also includes a one-and-a-half-acre native Iowa tree arboretum, with markers on trees to aid in their identification.

Distance: 1.4-mile lollipop
Approximate hiking time: 45 minutes to 1 hour
Difficulty: Easy. There is some woods hiking, but the trail is easy to follow.
Trail surface: Dirt and grass
Best seasons: Spring through fall
Other trail users: Cross-country skiers
Canine compatibility: Leashed dogs permitted
Fees and permits: None
Schedule: 6:30 a.m. to 10:30 p.m. daily spring through fall;
sunrise to sunset in winter
Maps: USGS Des Moines SE; trail map available from contact listed below
Trail contact: Polk County Conservation, 11407 NW Jester Park Dr., Granger 50109; (515) 323-5300; www.leadingyououtdoors .org
Special considerations: The trail can get muddy—good shoes are a necessity.
Other: Water and restrooms available in the park but not at the trailhead or along the trail

Finding the trailhead: Take I-35 to exit 68 (IA 5) and head east on IA 5. Drive 8 miles and take exit 96 (CR R63/SW 9th Street). After exiting, turn left, drive 1 mile and turn right onto County Line Road. Drive 1 mile and turn left onto 5th Street. Drive 0.5 mile to the park entrance on your left. The trail begins about 0.3 mile inside the park, on the left side of the park road after you drive past a picnic shelter, beyond a small gravel parking area. GPS: N41 31.167' / W93 36.738'

The Hike

The hike begins with a walk through a short stretch of woods. Wild raspberries sprout amidst the trees on this wide, emerald green path, and you soon reach the shore of the park's modest pond. Fishing is popular here, and you may spot a few anglers casting for bluegill and catfish. Breezes often blow gently across the waters, while Canada geese nibble in the grass along the banks—you can usually walk right up to them, if you'd like to take a photo.

The hike moves along the banks of the pond, which covers seven acres near the center of the park. Walking near the grassy banks, you will pass a large field of wildflowers, including numerous purple thistles, Queen Anne's lace, and black-eyed Susans. After coming around to the other side of the pond, enter another stretch of woods, which is dominated by many impressive oak and aspen trees.

The walk through the woods takes you along a short loop. Flowers on this stretch of the hike include fleabane and mullein. Deer are frequent visitors, skittering out from behind trees and racing across the path.

Exiting the woods, you come back alongside the pond. Retrace your steps from here to the trailhead.

If you want to check out the arboretum, it's a short drive from the trailhead, on the other side of the pond near a playground and picnic shelter. The stretch of pond bank near the arboretum has numerous wildflowers as well.

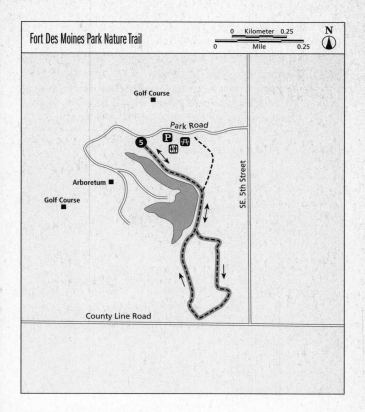

0   Kilometer   0.25

0   Mile   0.25

N

Golf Course

Park Road

5

P

A

SE. 5th Street

Arboretum

Golf Course

County Line Road

Miles and Directions

0.0   Start by walking into the woods and away from the parking area.

0.1   Reach the edge of the pond. Continue following the trail, walking with the pond on your right.

0.2   Reach a junction with a spur path that veers off to your left. Head right and continue walking with the pond on your right.

0.4 Reach another junction and follow the left fork into the woods. Shortly after, the path forks again—take the left fork and follow the path in a clockwise circle through the woods.

0.9 Reach another junction and veer to the left. Almost immediately, come to another fork and veer right. The pond comes into view through the trees on your left. Close the loop at the junction. From here, retrace your steps back to the start of the hike.

1.4 Arrive back at the trailhead.

6 Wymore Trail

New housing developments have sprouted in the open countryside around Easter Lake Park, in the southeastern corner of Des Moines, yet the Wymore Trail still offers a wilderness experience for those who make this short hike within sight of the park's 172-acre lake. The lake draws anglers with its stocks of bluegill, bullhead, catfish, crappie, bass, and walleye.

Distance: 0.7-mile loop

Approximate hiking time: 45 minutes to 1 hour

Difficulty: Moderate. There are several hills along the trail, as well as numerous spur paths off the main path, which can make for somewhat tricky navigation.

Trail surface: Dirt and grass

Best seasons: Spring through fall

Other trail users: Cross-country skiers

Canine compatibility: Leashed dogs permitted

Fees and permits: None

Schedule: 6:30 a.m. to 10:30 p.m. daily spring through fall; sunrise to sunset in winter

Maps: USGS Des Moines SE; trail map available from contacts listed below

Trail contacts: Easter Lake Park, 2830 Easter Lake Dr., Des Moines 50320; (515) 285-7612. Polk County Conservation, 11407 NW Jester Park Dr., Granger 50109; (515) 323-5300; www.leadingyououtdoors .org

Other: Horses prohibited; water and restroom available at trailhead

Finding the trailhead: From I-235, take exit 9 (US 69/East 14th Street), heading south. Drive 2.9 miles and veer left onto Indianola Avenue. Drive 1.5 miles and turn left onto Easter Lake Drive. Drive 1 mile to the park entrance on your left. Once you have entered

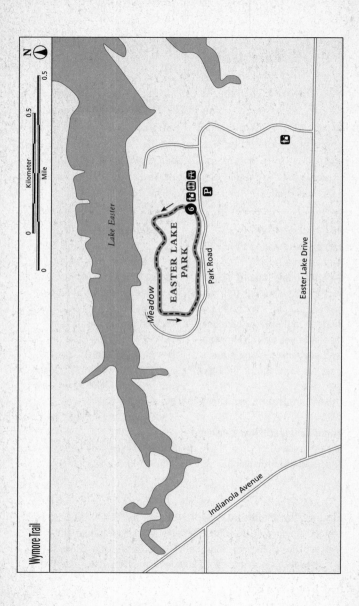

the park, pass a ranger station on your left and follow the left fork of the park road, then take another left fork and follow the road to picnic shelter 3. Park in spaces just past the shelter—the trailhead is just past the parking area, on the right side of the road. GPS: N41 32.479' / W93 33.951'

The Hike

As you start off on the hike, follow the path as it almost immediately plunges into rugged woods, with birds hopping and chirping in the trees. Deer tracks crisscross the path, although vehicles on nearby roads may keep the animals away during your hike.

The hike takes you over several small hills, with trees arching overhead. Look for the distinctive white, spiky flowers of horsemint growing alongside the path. Blue violet grows here as well. Stay alert as you're hiking—the spiderweb network of smaller paths that crisscrosses the main path, with many spurs heading toward the park's lake, can make following the route challenging in some places.

After crossing over two small creekbeds, you will eventually reach the west end of the lake, which is visible through the trees. If it's a sunny day, the lake is quite a sight, with the sun's rays glistening as they reflect off the waters. At this point, the path becomes wider and more grassy. Soon after, you come out of the woods and meet up with the park road, following it back to the trailhead. Along this stretch of road, the canopy of oak and other trees grows even thicker, making for an enjoyable ending to the hike.

You may want to check out the lake while you're here. Easter Lake Park was built on the site of the last operating coal mine in Polk County, and mine spoils are still visible in other parts of the park. The park also is home to the county's last remaining covered bridge, which was built in 1887 and moved to the park in 1967.

Miles and Directions

0.0 Start by walking from the trailhead into the woods and take the first right fork on the path. You will soon come to another fork in the trail—go left and continue on the main path.

0.1 Descend a hill, then follow the path around a sharp left turn. Ascend two slopes and cross a small creekbed.

0.2 Reach a fork in the trail. Veer right, then reach another fork and veer left.

0.3 Reach a T junction, with a meadow on your right. Turn left and follow the path, which soon merges with another path coming from the left. Reach a grassy area alongside the park road. Turn left and walk along the road back toward the trailhead.

0.7 Arrive back at the trailhead.

7 Eagle View and Pond Trails

Perched atop 150-foot bluffs looking out over the Des Moines River and surrounding countryside, Yellow Banks Park has a wealth of scenic overlooks, as well as trails leading to a Native American burial mound and huge savanna oaks. This short hike takes in two trails at the far end of the park, highlighted by a good spot to watch for the many migrating birds that pass by. Raptors are perhaps the most common— look for them in the spring and fall.

Distance: 0.7 mile out and back
Approximate hiking time: 30 to 45 minutes
Difficulty: Moderate, as the last part of the hike involves a climb up a hill
Trail surface: Dirt and grass
Best seasons: Spring through fall
Other trail users: None
Canine compatibility: Leashed dogs permitted
Fees and permits: None
Schedule: 6:30 a.m. to 10:30 p.m. daily spring through fall; sunrise to sunset in winter
Maps: USGS Rising Sun; trail map available from contacts listed below
Trail contacts: Yellow Banks Park, 6801 SE 32nd Ave., Des Moines 50317; (515) 266-1563. Polk County Conservation, 11407 NW Jester Park Dr., Granger 50109; (515) 323-5300; www.leadingyououtdoors.org
Other: Cyclists, horses, and snowmobiles prohibited

Finding the trailhead: From I-80, take exit 83 (US 65), heading south. Take exit 77 (SE Vandalia Road). At the end of the exit ramp turn right, then turn left onto SE Vandalia Road, heading east. Drive 2.5 miles to 68th Street and turn right onto SE 68th Street, crossing SE 32nd Street and heading into the park. Veer left at the roundabout, then drive 1 mile, passing a playground, campgrounds, and a ball field, to a fork in the road. Veer left at the fork—the hike begins shortly down the road on your right (look for the gap in the woods). GPS: N41 32.522' / W93 27.781'

The Hike

This "two-armed" hike begins with a short walk through the woods on the Eagle View Trail, leading to a bluff overlook that gives you a sweeping view of the Des Moines River valley to the west. This is a great spot for bird watching: In addition to raptors, scarlet and summer tanagers, eastern bluebirds, wintering bald eagles, and yellow-billed cuckoos have been spotted here, as have the occasional black-billed cuckoo, indigo bunting, and great-crested flycatcher.

Heading back to the park road, note the majestic oak trees along the path, which become even more numerous after you cross the road to the Pond Trail and begin a slow descent down the backside of the bluff. The yellow loess soil under the bluffs has yielded fossilized snail shells from the last ice age, and the park's Native American burial mound was created by the Woodland culture about AD 100.

As you continue toward the pond, the white and yellow flowers of daisy fleabane also sprout along the path, near the base of the tall trees. The path dead-ends on a thin, muddy spit by the five-acre pond. Frogs hop through the murky waters, and algae blooms around the shoreline.

From the pond, head back up the hill to the park road. If you have time, explore a bit of the rest of the park: The terrain presents good examples of savanna and the transition zone between prairie and forest, and the Savanna Trail takes a loop through rare savanna woodland.

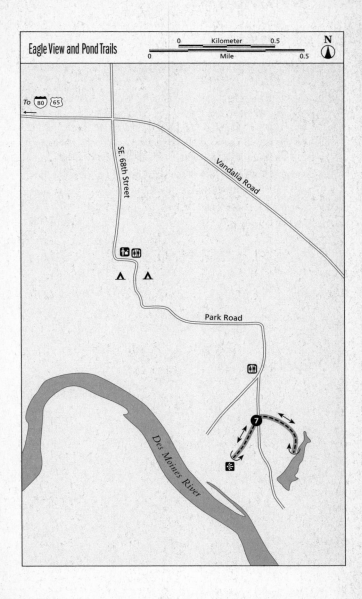

Eagle View and Pond Trails

N

| 0 | Kilometer | 0.5 |
| 0 | Mile | 0.5 |

To 80 65

SE. 68th Street

Vandalia Road

Park Road

Des Moines River

7

Miles and Directions

0.0 Start by walking into the woods on your right onto the Eagle View Trail.

0.1 Reach the overlook at the edge of the bluff. Turn around and return to the road, crossing to the other side and moving to your left to pick up the Pond Trail. Walk toward the woods on this side of the road, crossing the junction with another trail as you enter the woods, then beginning a descent.

0.5 Arrive at the pond. Turn around and head back uphill to the road. Then walk back to the trailhead.

0.7 Arrive back at the trailhead.

8 Trestle to Trestle Trail

With lots of neat little pools swarming with flora and fauna alongside the trail as it passes through boggy lowlands along the Des Moines River, this hike is a great opportunity to explore the natural world near the heart of the city. Moving southeast, this hike on a rails-to-trails conversion passes through largely undisturbed areas before abruptly coming to a busy stretch of road on the north side of Des Moines. The paved path also winds north toward Johnston, connecting to that suburb's trail system.

Distance: 3.2 miles out and back
Approximate hiking time: 1.5 to 2 hours
Difficulty: Easy (straight, flat surface)
Trail surface: Paved path
Best seasons: Spring through fall
Other trail users: Cyclists
Canine compatibility: Leashed dogs permitted
Fees and permits: None

Schedule: Sunrise to sunset daily
Maps: USGS Des Moines NW; trail map available from contact listed below
Trail contact: Polk County Conservation, 11407 NW Jester Park Dr., Granger 50109; (515) 323-5300; www.leadingyououtdoors .org
Special considerations: Pavement is cracked and eroding in places; watch your step

Finding the trailhead: From I-80/35, take exit 131 (IA 28/Merle Hay Road), heading south. Drive 0.5 mile and turn left on Meredith Drive, heading east. Drive 1 mile and turn left on Beaver Avenue, heading north. Drive 2 blocks and turn right onto Lower Beaver Drive, then drive 0.3 mile to the parking area and trailhead on your left. GPS: N41 38.810' / W93 40.429'

The Hike

As you begin your hike, note the green, sluggish river waters to your left. Lots of Queen Anne's lace, goldenrod, and horsemint blooms along the trail, and there are black-eyed Susans, too. Unlike some other lowland trails, the path is perched *above* the bottomlands along the river, keeping you out of the swampy terrain and at least somewhat removed from swarms of mosquitoes that may congregate there.

Shortly after starting out, you move away from main roads and into a much quieter stretch of path—although you're heading toward the center of the city, it feels like a remote, rural area. You'll walk rather close to the river; it's separated from the path by a strip of woods, but you can still see to the opposite bank, which is some distance across.

There's plenty of birdlife on this hike: Flocks of robins descend over the path, and cardinals flit among the trees. With lots of open space, you should get a good look at the birds, as well as have numerous photo opportunities.

Continue along with the river on your left, eventually reaching a large pond on your right, separated from the path by several rows of cattail. Lily pads are arrayed over the marshy waters, and the occasional frog breaks the surface to hop across the path. The sound of crickets and other insects pulses through the numerous clumps of wildflowers.

A row of power poles marching toward the horizon is the first sign you're heading back into civilization. A residential neighborhood and busy thoroughfare loom in the distance—this is where you turn around and head back to the starting point.

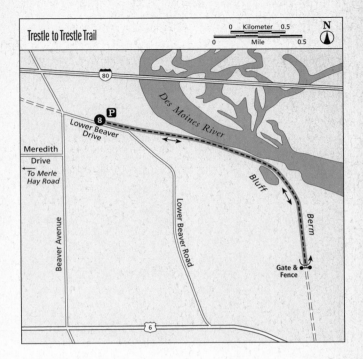

Miles and Directions

0.0 Begin by walking east, with a complex of gas pipes across the street on your right and the river bottom on your left. Come to a road, cross over, and move along the path into deeper tree cover.

0.5 Come alongside the river. Look to the left for the highway bridge in the distance.

0.9 A bluff on your right tapers off as you follow the path past a large pond.

1.3 Follow the path as it runs parallel with a gravel road on your right.

1.6 Reach a gate in a fence on your right, with a berm/levee on the left. Turn around and head back toward the trailhead.

3.2 Arrive back at the trailhead and parking area.

⑨ Summerset Trail

This hike takes in the north end of the Summerset Trail, which winds roughly a dozen miles total and includes a nice spot to view herons as they swoop over the open fields. The hike also features numerous wildflowers as the path moves through open countryside outside the town of Carlisle, south of Des Moines.

Distance: 6.8 miles out and back

Approximate hiking time: 3 to 3.5 hours

Difficulty: Moderate (smooth, flat surface but rather lengthy)

Trail surface: Paved path

Best seasons: Spring through fall

Other trail users: Cyclists, cross-country skiers

Canine compatibility: Leashed dogs permitted

Fees and permits: None

Schedule: Sunrise to sunset daily

Maps: USGS Hartford; trail map available from contact listed below

Trail contact: Warren County Conservation Board, 15565 118th Ave., Indianola 50125; (515) 961-6169; www .warrenccb.org

Other: Horses prohibited. The parking area at the trailhead has a picnic shelter and portable toilets but no water source. There is a convenience store/gas station right next to the trailhead parking area.

Finding the trailhead: From I-80 take exit 141 onto US 65. Drive 11 miles south on US 65 and take exit 72/IA 5 toward Carlisle. Drive about 2.3 miles on IA 5, crossing the North River and entering Carlisle. Just past the traffic light at 1st Street, turn right on 165th Place and park in the gravel parking lot at the trailhead. GPS: N41 29.602' / W93 29.156'

The Hike

The hike begins by following the path alongside marshy lowlands, with cattail sprouting up from standing water. Despite running alongside a two-lane country road and past new housing developments, the trail can be very quiet and peaceful, with nice views of the surrounding countryside. A creek gurgles just beyond the thick stands of grass at the edge of the path.

After crossing a bridge over the creek, you will begin to spot wildflowers on the trail's edge. Keep an eye out for blue iris and blue chicory. White herons soar over the open land on your right, which may have been a buffalo wallow back when this land was all open prairie. Purple spiderwort and white Canadian anemone are other flora you may see, as are yellowish clumps of wild parsnip and the distinctive three leaves of poison ivy—use caution if you step off the path.

Continue walking past rolling green hills as you cross several more creeks before turning around and heading back to the trailhead.

Option: You may continue hiking on the path for a couple more miles to Summerset State Park, which is located about halfway between the towns of Carlisle and Indianola.

Miles and Directions

0.0 Begin by walking down the paved path, with the parking area on your left and a trailer park on your right. Cross a small bridge over a creek.

0.3 Cross a road leading into the trailer park on your right. Continue on the path.

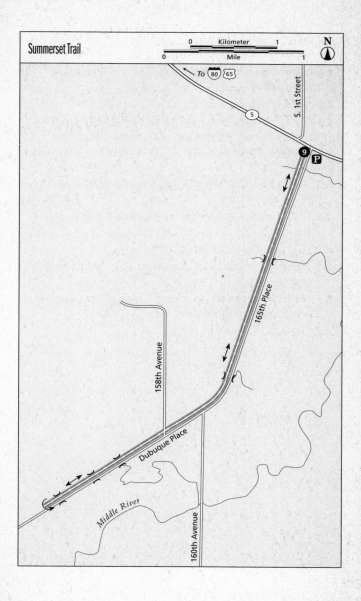

Summerset Trail

0   Kilometer   1

0   Mile   1

N

To 80 65

S. 1st Street

5

9 P

165th Place

158th Avenue

Dubuque Place

Middle River

160th Avenue

0.8 Cross a bridge over a creek, then cross a road leading into a housing development on your right.

1.4 Cross a driveway leading to a road on your left that runs parallel to the path.

1.7 Cross a bridge over a creek.

2.1 Cross a bridge over a creek opposite the intersection with 160th Avenue, and continue on the path. Just past this crossing, the creek on your left grows boggy and green with algae.

2.3 Reach the intersection of 158th Avenue and Dubuque Place. Cross a gravel road.

2.8 Reach a longer bridge over a creek. Cross over and continue on the path.

3.0 Cross another bridge over a creek.

3.3 Cross yet another bridge over a creek and continue on the path, passing under power lines.

3.4 Reach a tractor track that crosses the path. Turn around and head back to the trailhead.

6.8 Arrive back at the trailhead.

10 Woodland Mounds Preserve Trail

Following a twisting path that winds through thick woods and up and down several hills, this hike is quite a workout. Located down a single-lane gravel road in farmland several miles south of Des Moines, this 325-acre site was inhabited 3,000 years ago by Native Americans who constructed large earthen mounds for use as either burial sites or for religious ceremonies.

Distance: 2.0-mile lollipop

Approximate hiking time: 1 to 1.5 hours

Difficulty: More challenging. Just getting to the preserve can be an adventure, and the hike goes through rugged terrain.

Trail surface: Dirt

Best seasons: Spring through fall

Other trail users: Cross-country skiers

Canine compatibility: Leashed dogs permitted

Fees and permits: None

Schedule: 6:30 a.m. to 10 p.m. daily

Maps: USGS Milo; trail map available from contact listed below

Trail contact: Warren County Conservation Board, 15565 118th Ave., Indianola 50125; (515) 961-6169, www.warrenccb.org

Special considerations: The preserve is at the end of a rugged gravel road—take it easy as you drive in.

Other: Pit latrines available at the parking area, but there is no water. Horses are prohibited. The preserve is used for hunting during hunting season—call beforehand to make sure that won't interfere with your hike.

Finding the trailhead: From IA 5 in Des Moines, take exit 70 (US 65/69) and drive south toward Indianola. After driving 10 miles, you have entered Indianola; turn left onto IA 92. Drive 4.5 miles and turn right onto 173rd Street. The junction is just before IA 92 enters the town of Ackworth; you are now on a gravel road. Drive 1 mile and turn left onto S23 Highway. (This is a paved road; it may be marked as Kennedy Street at the turn.) Drive 1 mile, crossing the South River, and turn left onto Keokuk Street. (NOTE: It's easy to miss this turn; pay close attention!) Follow Keokuk Street for 1 mile, then continue on the road as it veers right and becomes 193rd Avenue, then almost immediately veers left and becomes Kirkwood Street. The preserve entrance is just ahead on your left—a sign with the number "19587" is at the turnoff. Follow the single-lane gravel road to the dirt and gravel parking area. The trail begins past the parking area, far to the right of the latrine and fire pit. GPS: N41 20.734' / W93 25.905'

The Hike

It's incredibly quiet in this preserve—you may be one of the only hikers here, and sounds are limited to tractors in the nearby fields and the calls of birds and insects. The path begins on a gradual descent, moving through the thick, thick woods, with the occasional spiderweb strung from trees or plants.

The tree cover is so thick that acorns nearly carpet the path in some places. Zipping through a couple of switchbacks, you eventually cross a bridge over a creekbed choked with tree trunks. The path then follows another hairpin turn and crosses another bridge over the same creek. The path can get muddy here!

From these lowlands, follow the path as it heads uphill. The trees provide good cover from the sun on hot days, as well as plenty of hiding places for deer—you may scare a few off the path! After coming to a junction, veer left, moving onto the "lollipop" section of the trail as you follow the

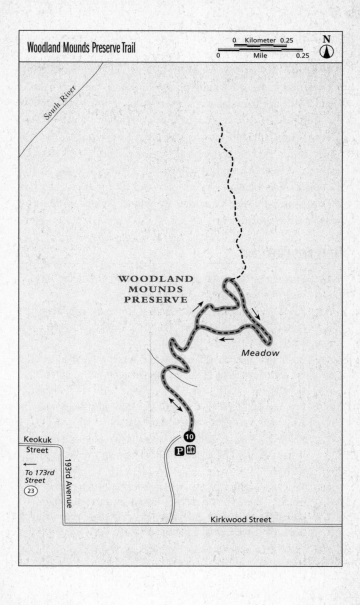

Woodland Mounds Preserve Trail

0   Kilometer   0.25
0   Mile   0.25

N

South River

WOODLAND
MOUNDS
PRESERVE

Meadow

Keokuk
Street

To 173rd
Street
(23)

193rd Avenue

10

P

Kirkwood Street

path through a small glade, then back into the woods and along a ridge atop a small ravine.

Moving along the ridge, sunlight finally begins to peek through the treetops—keep an ear open for the bird calls as well. Swinging back around and heading south back toward the trailhead, come to a large, grassy meadow just before veering right and plunging again into deep woods.

Another descent closes the lollipop. After you retrace your route to the creek, the trail climbs uphill back to the trailhead. Wildflowers aren't plentiful along this trail, but if you look carefully you may spot some sweet william or other native species.

Miles and Directions

0.0   Start out by taking the unmarked path that runs to the left. Walk into the woods.

0.2   Follow the path as it takes a gradual turn to the right, then moves through switchbacks and crosses a bridge over a creek. Cross the creek again on a second bridge.

0.6   Come to a junction with another unmarked path. Veer to the left and move along the path. This is the beginning of the "lollipop."

0.9   Veer and follow the path to your right. Immediately come to a junction. Veer right and follow the path.

1.1   Reach the edge of the woods, with a meadow spread out in front of you. Turn right and follow the path through the woods.

1.4   Arrive back at the junction where you took the left path, closing the loop of the lollipop. Take a left and follow the path back downhill to the bridges over the creek, then uphill toward the trailhead and parking area.

2.0   Arrive back at the trailhead and parking area.

11 Carney Marsh Trail

Nestled between two major highways and just a stone's throw from a small airport, Carney Marsh is a natural gem on the outskirts of the rapidly growing Des Moines suburb of Ankeny: a forty-acre native wetland and prairie with a wealth of wildlife-spotting opportunities, especially of seasonal birds that camouflage themselves in thick tree cover. Although this is a fairly short, straight trail, you may very well end up spending hours here just trying to spot the many birds and waterfowl that roost in the trees and swampy pools alongside the path.

Distance: 2.0 miles out and back
Approximate hiking time: 1 to 1.5 hours
Difficulty: Easy (straight and flat)
Trail surface: Paved path
Best seasons: Spring through fall
Other trail users: Cyclists
Canine compatibility: Leashed dogs permitted
Fees and permits: None

Schedule: 6:30 a.m. to 10:30 p.m. daily; closes at sunset in winter
Map: USGS Des Moines NE
Trail contact: Polk County Conservation, 11407 NW Jester Park Dr., Granger 50109; (515) 323-5300; www.leadingyououtdoors .org
Special considerations: Do not feed wildlife at the marsh.

Finding the trailhead: From I-35 heading north from Des Moines, take exit 89 (Corporate Woods Drive/NE 66th Avenue). At the end of the ramp, turn left and head west on NE 66th Avenue. Drive 1 mile and turn right onto NE 14th Street/US 69. Drive 1 long block and turn right onto NE 70th Street, then drive 0.5 mile to the parking area for the trail on your left. GPS: N41 41.307' / W93 35.456'

The Hike

The path runs right alongside Carney Marsh, with the occasional bench along the way to give you a spot to stop and watch the wildlife. Cattails grow high and thick at the edge of the marsh, as do several varieties of wildflowers, including purple coneflower. In some spots water comes right up to the edge of the path, and also rushes through inlets overgrown with foliage.

Shortly after starting out on your hike, the open water of the pond that is home to ducks and other waterfowl gives way to green marshy lowlands, well shaded by large trees. The trail then shifts habitats yet again, entering a more woodsy area, with trunks clustered along the path and dead limbs littering the ground. The canopy of trees grows even thicker as you hike past housing units built just off the trail.

Throughout the hike, keep an eye out for birds: Bluebirds, robins, and swallows are just some of the species you may spot flapping their wings through the trees. Frogs also use the path as a shortcut from the main marsh to the standing sloughs on the other side of the path. You may also spot some old railroad debris off to your left—tracks still run through this area.

If you're hiking in the fall, keep an eye out for muskrat lodges. Constructed out of thick clumps of cattail and other marsh plants, the distinctive lodges are fairly visible throughout the marsh. Canada geese use the lodges as nesting sites in the spring, which is also breeding time for ring-tailed pheasants. Raptors soar overhead, their impressive wingspans making them easy to spot.

After passing a few more spots of sluggish water, as well as some algae-choked pools on the fringes of the marsh,

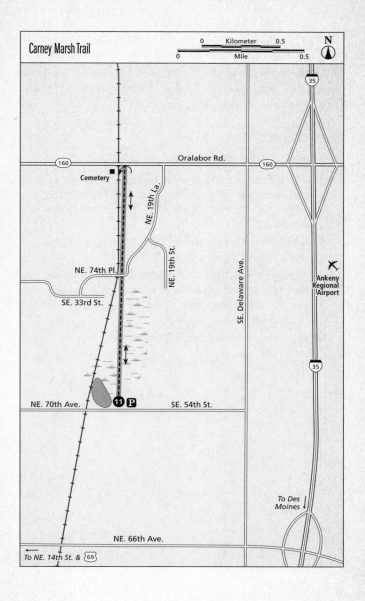

Carney Marsh Trail

Kilometer
0   0.5
Mile
0   0.5

N

Oralabor Rd.

160   160

Cemetery

NE. 19th La.

NE. 19th St.

NE. 74th Pl.

SE. 33rd St.

SE. Delaware Ave.

Ankeny
Regional
Airport

35

11 P

NE. 70th Ave.   SE. 54th St.

To Des
Moines

35

NE. 66th Ave.

To NE. 14th St. & 69

you will reach Oralabor Road, a major thoroughfare on the southern edge of Ankeny, with a cemetery off to the left. This is the turnaround point. The walk back to the trailhead will almost certainly give you just as many opportunities to look for interesting flora and fauna.

Miles and Directions

0.0 Start by walking with the marsh and pond on your left.

0.3 After passing by the open water, look to your left for rows of large trees over the marsh. The marsh opens up on the right side of the path here as well. Houses soon loom into view on your left.

0.5 Reach the intersection with NE 74th Place. Cross over and continue walking on the path.

1.0 A cemetery is located off to the left of the trail. Follow the path as it exits the woods and reaches the railroad tracks next to Oralabor Road. Turn around and head back toward the trailhead.

2.0 Arrive back at the trailhead and parking area.

12 Hickory Ridge Trail

Running alongside a small stream through a wooded ravine, this is one of several fine trails in Jester Park, one of Polk County's best nature and recreation areas. Stretching for nearly 2,000 acres on the west shore of Saylorville Lake, north of Des Moines, Jester Park is a mecca for birders: The park is listed as a globally significant bird area by the American Bird Conservancy, and is a major migration stopover for the American white pelican—some 3,000 to 8,000 of them pass through beginning in late August and peaking around Labor Day. Gulls and waterfowl come through later in the year.

Distance: 1.2 miles out and back

Approximate hiking time: 1 hour

Difficulty: Moderate due to a few small hills

Trail surface: Dirt

Best seasons: Spring through fall

Other trail users: Cross-country skiers

Canine compatibility: Leashed dogs permitted

Fees and permits: None

Schedule: 6:30 a.m. to 10:30 p.m. daily; closes at sunset in winter

Maps: USGS Granger; trail map available from contact listed below

Trail contact: Polk County Conservation, 11407 NW Jester Park Dr., Granger 50109; (515) 323-5300; www.leadingyouout doors.org

Other: Cyclists and horses prohibited. Water and restrooms are available in the park, but not at the trailhead or along the trail.

Finding the trailhead: Take I-80/35 to exit 127 (IA 141), heading north. Drive 6.8 miles on IA 141 and turn right on NW 121st Street. Drive 2.1 miles and turn right on NW 118th Avenue, then drive 0.6 mile, veering onto the left fork, to the park entrance. Follow the park road as it curves to the left and drive 1 mile, with the lake on your right. Just after reaching the campground registration hut, veer left and drive 0.8 mile, with the golf course on your left, to reach the trailhead, which has a sign and a small parking area. GPS: N41 47.095' / W93 47.283'

The Hike

From the beginning of the hike, you pass impressive cottonwood and hickory trees along the path. This is a heavily wooded area, and birds, including song sparrows, chirp in the trees. After a short descent, follow the trail as it runs alongside a stream on the left, with a large bluff arching overhead.

The tree cover grows even thicker as you continue, with sunlight only occasionally stabbing through. Clusters of wild mushrooms grow up along the trail in several hues, including white, brown, and reddish-purple. Acorns scatter across the path, and snails work their way into the ground.

Following the trail past a couple of spur trails, you eventually come to a very impressive cottonwood tree. (You'll know it when you see it.) The tree stands in the bottomlands of Saylorville Lake, and its trunk will probably be underwater if the area has had recent heavy rainfall—in fact, the path gets washed out at this point as water from the lake spills over into the park.

Beyond the cottonwood, the path reaches the park road. Along this stretch is a children's natural play area and a bison and elk corral that has been here nearly four decades. This is the turnaround point.

Option: Heading back to the trailhead, you may want to take a short side hike by turning at the junction closest

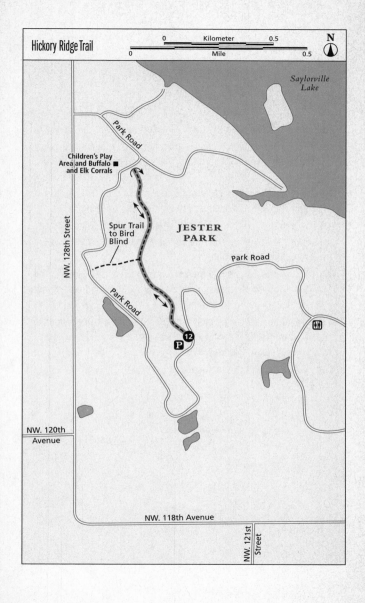

Hickory Ridge Trail

0   Kilometer   0.5

0   Mile   0.5

N

Saylorville Lake

Park Road

Children's Play Area and Buffalo and Elk Corrals

JESTER PARK

Spur Trail to Bird Blind

Park Road

NW. 128th Street

Park Road

P 12

NW. 120th Avenue

NW. 118 Avenue

NW. 121st Street

to the trailhead, where the trail crosses the stream to a small bird blind. This additional hike is about 0.1 mile each way and takes about a half hour.

Miles and Directions

0.0   Begin by following the path as it descends into the woods.

0.2   Follow the trail as it climbs a small hill, moving slightly away from the stream on your left. There is a bench at the top of the hill.

0.3   Descend to a T junction at the bottom of the hill. Take the right fork and follow the path as it climbs another hill.

0.4   Reach the top of the hill and another junction. Take the left fork. Shortly after, the trail curves slightly to the right and runs just below a small ridge.

0.5   Follow the trail as it slopes downward to a small slough. This area floods after heavy rains. A huge cottonwood tree stands at this point.

0.6   Reach the park road that runs by the buffalo and elk corrals and the children's play area. Turn around and retrace your route back to the trailhead.

1.2   Arrive back at the trailhead.

13 Jack Pine Trail

A nearly 9,000-acre wildlife refuge that has grown up along formerly drained areas by the South Skunk River, Chichaqua Bottoms Greenbelt is crisscrossed by oxbow channels that flow through a landscape of restored wetlands, savanna, and woodlands. The refuge is home to numerous animal species: River otters were reintroduced here in 1997, and ornate box turtles in 1998. A nearby area is devoted to sandhill cranes.

The park has a good selection of trails, providing lots of hiking through lowland areas along the oxbows. It can get muddy along the Jack Pine and other trails, but it's well worth the opportunity to see a wide variety of wildlife.

Distance: 1.3-mile loop
Approximate hiking time: 1 hour
Difficulty: Moderate due to trail sections that can be overgrown and/or muddy, especially after heavy rains
Trail surface: Dirt and grass
Best seasons: Spring through fall
Other trail users: Cross-country skiers
Canine compatibility: Leashed dogs permitted
Fees and permits: None
Schedule: 6:30 a.m. to 10:30 p.m. daily; closes at sunset in winter
Map: USGS Loring
Trail contacts: Chichaqua

Bottoms Greenbelt, 8600 NE 126th Ave., Maxwell 50161; (515) 967-2596. Polk County Conservation, 11407 NW Jester Park Drive, Granger 50109; (515) 323-5300; www.leadingyououtdoors.org
Special considerations: Sections of the park, including some hiking trails, are closed for hunting from dates in September through November. Contact the park or conservation board for details. Trails can get muddy or flood after heavy rains and trail routes may change due to work at the park; again, check for details before you head out.

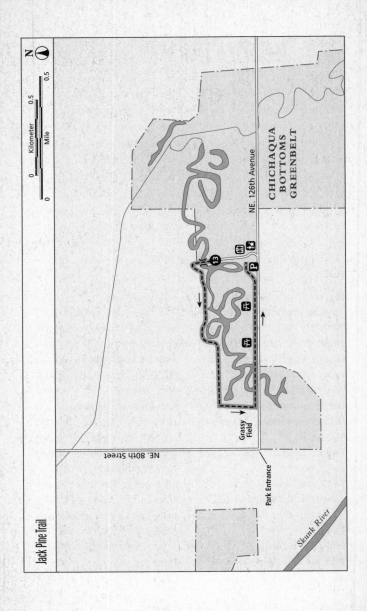

Jack Pine Trail

N

0   Kilometer   0.5
0   Mile   0.5

NE. 126th Avenue

CHICHAQUA
BOTTOMS
GREENBELT

13

P

Grassy
Field

NE. 80th Street

Park Entrance

Skunk River

Finding the trailhead: From I-80 heading east from Des Moines, take exit 142 (US 65/Hubbell Avenue, heading northeast toward Bondurant). Drive 2 miles to Grant Street and turn left. Drive for 9 miles along Grant Street; the road eventually becomes NE 72nd Street, then curves right and becomes Yoder Drive before straightening and becoming NE 134th Avenue. Turn right on NE 80th Street and drive 1 mile to the park entrance, turning left onto NE 126th Street. Follow NE 126th Street about 1 mile to a parking area on your left, next to a Quonset hut "long house." The ranger station is just past the parking area, and the trailhead is a little farther inside the park, past the campsites and by the bridge over the old channel of the Skunk River. GPS: N41 47.636' / W93 25.772'

The Hike

The hike begins as you cross the historic, 100-foot, early Warren truss bridge spanning the old channel of the Skunk River, the longest bridge of its kind in Iowa. Green algae blooms in swampy pools along the trail on the far side of the bridge, and water may come well up over tree trunks during the rainy season.

Moving along, you get a sense of the wide variety of habitats in the greenbelt. The trail runs briefly through woodland, but then swings past an open field thick with tallgrass. Wild raspberries can be seen alongside the path. Swamp milkweed and hoary vervain are some of the other flora that blooms in the park.

The swampy surroundings continue, with frogs hopping across the path and through the thick grasses on their way to pools alongside the river. Different species of turtle and snake call the park home as well—if it's quiet enough, you may hear them moving through the overgrowth around the river.

Moving through more woods, you pick up the sounds of birds: Over 200 species are here, including the rose-breasted grosbeak, common yellowthroat, and seventeen types of sparrow, including lark and swamp sparrows.

Exiting the woods, you make your way back to the trail-head along the park road. Stay alert along this portion of the hike—you may catch sight of a lone heron arcing over the low, flat wetlands. Both the green heron and black-crowned night heron have been spotted here. Arriving back at the ranger station, you may want to rent a canoe to further explore the oxbows!

Miles and Directions

0.0 Start by crossing the bridge and following the path into the woods, crossing under a large fallen tree.

0.1 Continue with the river on your left. The woods thin out somewhat.

0.3 The path reenters a wooded area. The river is still on your left as the path curves to the left, then to the right, then runs for a long straightaway.

0.6 Follow the path as it curves left, coming very close to the river. The path then runs into a grassy field, with the river still on your left.

0.7 Exit the woods and come out at the park road. Turn left to follow the road back to the ranger station. Cross over the river as you head back toward the office.

1.3 Arrive back at the office/parking area.

14 Chichaqua Valley Trail

A former rail line used by several different railroads, this popular hiking and cycling trail cuts across the southeast corner of Chichaqua Bottoms Greenbelt and runs for nearly 20 miles from just outside the town of Bondurant to Baxter, passing through other towns along the way. This hike begins surrounded by cornfields, but quickly moves into the woods that run along the bottomlands near the Skunk River. Santiago Creek threads its way along the trail as well.

Distance: 4.6 miles out and back

Approximate hiking time: 2 to 2.5 hours

Difficulty: Moderate; a largely flat route, but somewhat long

Trail surface: Paved path

Best seasons: Spring through fall

Other trail users: Cyclists

Canine compatibility: Leashed dogs permitted

Fees and permits: None

Schedule: 6:30 a.m. to 10:30 p.m. daily spring through fall; sunrise to sunset in winter

Maps: USGS Altoona; trail map available from contact listed below

Trail contact: Polk County Conservation, 11407 NW Jester Park Dr., Granger 50109; (515) 323-5300; www.leadingyououtdoors .org. (Co-managed with Jasper County Conservation.)

Special considerations: Flooding is a possibility along this trail after heavy rains; call beforehand to check conditions.

Other: Horses prohibited. A portable toilet is available at trailhead, but there is no water.

Finding the trailhead: From I-80 heading east of Des Moines, take exit 142 (US 65). Drive 5 miles northeast on US 65, passing through the town of Bondurant, and turn right onto 88th Street. Drive 0.5 mile to the paved parking lot and trailhead on your left. GPS: N41 42.466' / W93 25.483'

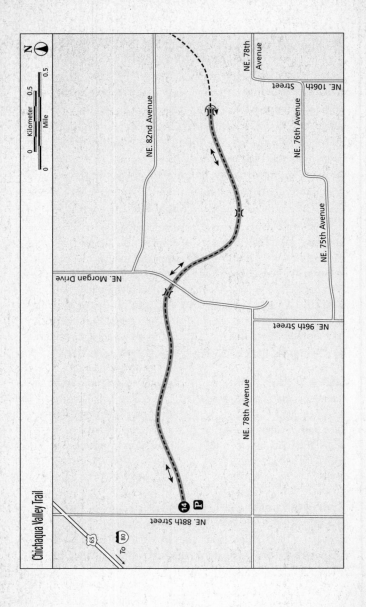

Chichaqua Valley Trail

NE. 82nd Avenue

NE. Morgan Drive

NE. 78th Avenue

NE. 96th Street

NE. 88th Street

To 80 65

14 P

N

Kilometer 0 0.5

Mile 0 0.5

NE. 78th Avenue

NE. 106th Street

NE. 76th Avenue

NE. 75th Avenue

The Hike

From the trailhead, near which stand a few apple trees, follow the path as it moves into the woods, which are bordered on either side by farm fields. Butterflies are plentiful on this hike, and you may catch sight of a bluebird or two moving through the trees. Stray corncobs and toadstools litter the path, and the hum of traffic can be heard from the nearby highway. You also may be able to pick up the sound of wild turkeys gobbling away in the woods—they roost in the nearby Chichaqua Bottoms Greenbelt and surrounding area.

You soon get your first view of Santiago Creek off to your right as it flows toward the nearby South Skunk River. Eventually, the creek becomes larger and faster, with frogs hopping in and out of the water that pools on the banks. The woods thin out a bit. Pass some open fields before coming to a bridge that marks the turnaround point of the hike. Head back, seeing if you can count all the creek views on your return!

Miles and Directions

0.0 Begin by walking along the path away from the parking area.

0.5 As you follow a long, looping right bend in the path, note the steep drop-off on both sides.

0.8 Follow the path on a long, looping left bend.

1.1 Walk across a bridge that spans Santiago Creek. Shortly afterward, cross NE Morgan Drive.

1.4 Cross a small bridge over the creek.

1.7 Cross a bridge over the creek.

2.3 Cross a bridge over Santiago Creek. Turn around and head back toward the trailhead.

4.6 Arrive back at the trailhead and parking area.

15 Heart of Iowa Nature Trail

Beginning in the town of Slater, this hike takes you into flat farmland north of Des Moines. The occasional tree and sprinkling of wildflowers provide welcome relief and diversion, respectively, if you are hiking this trail on a hot summer day. A short drive to the west of the Slater trailhead is the High Trestle Trail, and plans are underway to connect this planned 32-mile trail to other trails as well, forming a 100-mile loop of trails in central Iowa.

Distance: 3.4 miles out and back

Approximate hiking time: 1.5 to 2 hours

Difficulty: Easy (straight, flat path)

Trail surface: Crushed limestone

Best seasons: Spring through fall

Other trail users: Cyclists, horseback riders, snowmobilers

Canine compatibility: Leashed dogs permitted

Fees and permits: None

Schedule: 5 a.m. to 10:30 p.m. daily

Maps: USGS Slater; trail map available from contact listed below. (Trail map also posted at trailhead.)

Trail contact: Story County Conservation Board, 56461 180th St., Ames 50010; (515) 232-2516; www .storycounty.com/index .aspx?DN=15,6,1,Documents

Other: Water and portable toilets available at the trailhead

Finding the trailhead: Take I-35 north out of Des Moines, then take exit 102 (IA 210), heading west. Drive for 6 miles to the town of Slater. At the intersection with CR R38/Linn Street, turn right. Drive 5 blocks, passing a school on your right along the way, and reach Trailhead Park & Arboretum and the parking area for the trail, on your right. The trailhead is just to the north of the parking area, next to the picnic shelter. GPS: N41 53.106' / W93 40.677'

The Hike

Before beginning your hike, take time to look around the small arboretum at the trailhead—trees showcased here include the linden, bur oak, and redbud. Setting off on the path, you may catch sight of birds soaring over the cornfields that line both sides of the trail. Cyclists zip by, taking advantage of the long, flat stretches on the path.

Soon a row of large, evenly spaced oak trees appears on the right side of the trail. The rows of corn seem unending, and barns and silos look especially striking against the spare, empty horizon. Try walking this trail at sunrise or sunset if you want to see some archetypal Iowa vistas! Keep an eye out for crop dusters as well, with their wings dipping as they pass over the cornfields.

Trees become less and less common as you move along the path. It can get pretty hot on this hike in the summer months with the lack of shade, which makes it a nice hike to do first thing in the morning or late in the afternoon. As far as you can see, the land is flat and covered with corn, although you may spot a patch of mullein or other wildflowers closer to the edge of the path.

The turnaround point is a shady clump of trees, a nice place to stop and rest before heading back to the trailhead. If you're hiking near the end of the day, keep your ears open for crickets chirping in the fields.

Miles and Directions

0.0 Begin by turning right and following the trail to the east, with the school complex in the field off to your right.

0.4 Pass a group of evenly spaced oak trees along the right side of the path.

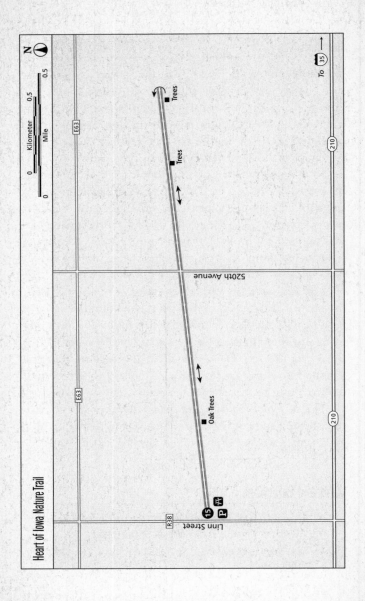

Heart of Iowa Nature Trail

N

Kilometer
0   0.5

Mile
0   0.5

Linn Street   R38

15   P   🚻

Oak Trees

520th Avenue

Trees

Trees

E63

E63

210

210

35
To

1.0 Come to an intersection with 520th Avenue. Cross over and continue on the path.

1.5 After passing an open stretch on the right side of the path, begin walking through a stretch shaded by trees.

1.7 Come to another clump of trees shading the path on your right. This is the turnaround point—head back from here to the trailhead.

3.4 Arrive back at the trailhead.

16 High Trestle Trail

Formerly known as the Ankeny-to-Woodward Trail, this path stretches 25 miles from the rapidly growing northern suburbs of Des Moines out into the countryside. While one leg of the trail heads west to a newly built bridge over the Des Moines River, scheduled to open in 2011, this hike follows another leg of the trail south from the town of Slater through a bucolic landscape of Iowa cornfields and small-town grain elevators.

Distance: 3.6 miles out and back

Approximate hiking time: 1.5 to 2 hours

Difficulty: Easy (flat, straight trail)

Trail surface: Paved path

Best seasons: Spring through fall

Other trail users: Cyclists, inline skaters

Canine compatibility: Leashed dogs permitted

Fees and permits: None

Schedule: 6:30 a.m. to 10:30 p.m. daily spring through fall; sunrise to sunset in winter

Maps: USGS Slater; USGS Polk City. Trail map available from contact listed below.

Trail contact: Polk County Conservation, 11407 NW Jester Park Dr., Granger 50109; (515) 323-5300; www.leadingyououtdoors .org

Other: Horses prohibited

Finding the trailhead: Take I-35 north out of Des Moines, then take exit 102 (IA 210), heading west. Drive for 6 miles to the town of Slater and the intersection with CR R38/Linn Street. Continue straight on IA 210 for 0.3 mile and turn right on Boone Street. Drive for 2 blocks and turn left onto 4th Avenue. Drive 2 blocks into Earl Grimm Park and park in the far end of the parking lot. The trail is at the edge of the park, past the baseball diamonds. GPS: N41 52.739' / W93 41.352'

The Hike

The hike starts out on the edge of Slater's main park and recreation complex, across town from the trailhead for the Heart of Iowa Nature Trail. Be careful not to take the path that circles the park—you want the path that moves away from the park, heading toward the highway through Slater.

Once on the trail, you're in the cornfields. Crickets chirp in the fields, and you'll probably spot farmers at work if your hike falls during the harvest season. (Be sure to pick up a few ears of sweet corn at one of the ubiquitous roadside stands while you're in the area.)

The corn grows high as you move along, and cyclists zip by on the path. Keep an eye out for the occasional wild raspberry bush, as well as numerous wildflowers, including the tall, yellow stalks of mullein, sweet-smelling horsemint, and purple clover.

The sky is big and blue on clear days from spring until fall, and thick tree limbs festooned with leaves offer some shade from the sun, including the drooping branches of willows. Take a look around at the vast vistas of farm fields stretching to the horizon, and keep an eye out for the grasshoppers and butterflies that flit along the path. There's even the occasional frog heading for low-lying ditches where water pools at the edge of the fields.

Passing through the quiet town of Sheldahl, you come to another stretch of fields and trees, with birds hopping in their branches. A road paralleling the trail south of Sheldahl marks the turnaround spot; head back to the trailhead from here.

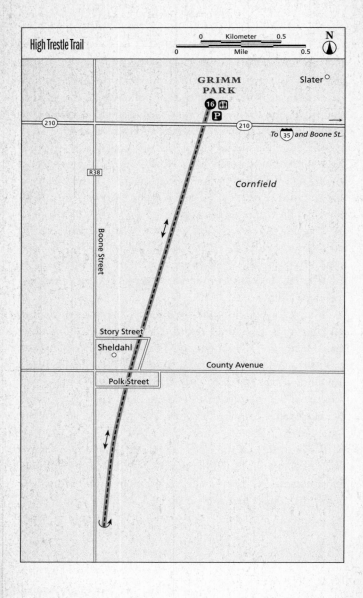

High Trestle Trail

0   Kilometer   0.5

0   Mile   0.5

N

GRIMM
PARK

16

P

Slater

210

210

To 35 and Boone St.

R38

Cornfield

Boone Street

Story Street

Sheldahl

County Avenue

Polk Street

Miles and Directions

0.0 Begin by walking away from the trailhead and park and toward the main road through Slater (IA 210). Cross the road, watching for traffic, and continue walking on the path.

0.4 Pass by the southern edge of Slater as it fades into a cornfield on your left.

1.0 Cross Story Street as you enter the town of Sheldahl.

1.2 Moving through Sheldahl, cross County Avenue and Polk Street, then follow the path as it moves out of town.

1.8 Continue walking on the path until you come within sight of Boone Street paralleling the trail. Turn around and head back to the trailhead.

3.6 Arrive back at the trailhead.

17 Hidden Prairie Nature Trail

More of a stroll than a true hike, this trail is located in Kuehn Conservation Area, a hidden gem of a park located quite a ways to the west of Des Moines, down several miles of gravel farm roads. Those who make the trek out here will be rewarded with a site that features both bucolic prairie and forest, home to deer and other wildlife.

Distance: 0.3-mile loop

Approximate hiking time: 30 minutes

Difficulty: Easy

Trail surface: Grass and dirt

Best seasons: Spring through fall

Other trail users: Cross-country skiers

Canine compatibility: Leashed dogs permitted

Fees and permits: None

Schedule: Sunrise to 10 p.m. daily spring through fall; sunrise to sunset in winter

Maps: USGS Redfield; USGS Adel. Trail map available from contact listed below.

Trail contact: Dallas County Conservation Board, 14581 K Ave., Perry 50220; (515) 465-3577; www.conservation.co .dallas.ia.us

Special considerations: The trail is a bit overgrown in places—make sure you know the route back.

Other: Restrooms available at nature center by trailhead

Finding the trailhead: Drive west from Des Moines on I-80 and take exit 106 (Dallas CR P58), heading north. Shortly after exiting, turn left on 352nd Place. Drive 1 mile to a T junction and turn right onto Jewell Drive, heading north. Follow Jewell Drive for 0.5 mile and stay on the road as it veers left and becomes Bear Creek Drive. Drive 2 miles on Bear Creek Drive, passing through the intersection with I Avenue and following the road as it bends right and becomes Houston Trail. (Do not follow Bear Creek Drive as it bends left.) Drive

2 more miles into the park, and park in the lot inside the entrance on your right. The trail begins just past the parking area. GPS: N41 33.797' / W94 07.883'

The Hike

Walking past tallgrass on the right, you head toward the forest, which is perched on a bluff above the South Raccoon River. The hike follows the boundary between prairie and woodland, moving around the thick stand of tallgrass—the grass is so thick that deer may be hiding in it and you will have no idea they are even there.

Numerous migrating birds make a stop in the park as well, including sparrows, warblers, and flycatchers. Bobolinks and bluebirds also have been spotted here, and owls hoot in the trees after sunset—nighttime is actually a good time to make this hike, as the remote park has spectacular views of the night sky, with the entire panorama of constellations spread out above.

Continue walking between the woods and prairie, which features different-colored wildflowers, including some large and distinctive black-eyed Susans. Have a look into the forest—it's carpeted with pine needles from the thick growth of pine trees that grow along the boundary of the park.

The path passes a barbed wire fence on your left, marking the edge of the park, then you reach the main park road, which you follow back to the parking area. From here, you may want to meander down to the sandbars on the river, where the belted kingfisher may be seen flitting along the water.

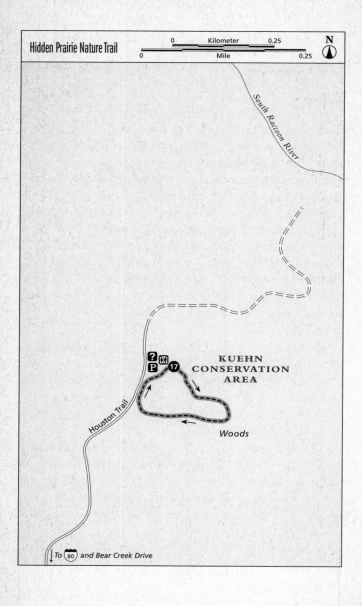

Hidden Prairie Nature Trail

0   Kilometer   0.25
0   Mile   0.25

N

South Raccoon River

KUEHN
CONSERVATION
AREA

P   17

Houston Trail

Woods

To 80 and Bear Creek Drive

Miles and Directions

0.0 Begin by taking the path that veers to your right. Walk along the path with the woods on your left, traveling the loop in a clockwise direction.

0.1 Swing around a clump of trees in the middle of the trail and continue walking on the path. Soon you will pass another path that forks off to the right—keep walking straight.

0.3 Walk past a barbed wire fence on your left, then reach the park road. Turn right and take a short walk back to the parking area and trailhead.

18 Hanging Rock Trail

This hike begins with the impressive sight of a huge outcrop of sandstone arching over the Middle Raccoon River. The surrounding park, tucked away on a side street in the town of Redfield, includes landscapes of wetlands, prairie, and woods, and the confluence of two tributaries of the Raccoon River is less than a mile downstream from the trailhead.

Distance: 1.0 mile out and back
Approximate hiking time: 40 minutes to 1 hour
Difficulty: Easy (flat, smooth surface)
Trail surface: Paved path
Best seasons: Spring through fall
Other trail users: Cyclists
Canine compatibility: Leashed dogs permitted
Fees and permits: None
Schedule: 8 a.m. to 10 p.m. daily spring through fall; 8 a.m.
to 5 p.m. in winter. The park may close due to weather conditions in winter.
Maps: USGS Redfield. Trail map may be available from contact listed below.
Trail contact: Dallas County Conservation Board, 14581 K Ave., Perry 50220; (515) 465-3577; www.conservation.co .dallas.ia.us
Other: Restrooms available in the park but not at the trailhead

Finding the trailhead: Drive west from Des Moines on I-80. Take exit 100 (Eldorado Avenue/Dallas CR F60) and drive north 5 miles, crossing over the South Raccoon River on the way (the road becomes El Paso Avenue), then reach the town limits of Redfield. Take the left fork of the road (First Street) into town, take the next fork to the left (Second Street), then turn left onto Redfield Street. Drive 1 block to the park entrance on your left. Follow the park road as it winds 0.5 mile to the rock outcrop and a parking area at the end of the road. GPS: N41 34.994' / W94 12.032'

The Hike

This paved path runs through thick woods that are naturally home to a variety of birds—listen for their calls as you move down the trail. Flowers along this stretch include the gray-headed coneflower.

Follow the path as it comes alongside the park road on your right. Keep your eyes peeled for the small opening through the trees on your left that leads to a river overlook. The path runs along the road, with an occasional glimpse through the trees to the river. You may spot a great blue heron as it skims over the water. Ospreys and bald eagles have also been seen in this area.

The path then moves into an overgrown prairie landscape, with a plethora of plant life, before winding around a few lazy curves and ending at a residential neighborhood. This is the turnaround point.

Arriving back at the rock outcrop, take a moment to study how the light plays across the rock face. Depending on the time of day, there may be some interesting shadows. Just downstream, the river flows over some gentle drop-offs.

Option: For a longer hike, you may want to continue past the turnaround point on the Hanging Rock Trail; it's just a 1-block walk up a small incline to an intersection with the Raccoon River Valley Trail, another nice hiking path.

Miles and Directions

0.0 Start by walking north with the rock outcrop and river on your left.

0.2 Pass a parking lot on your left and continue to follow the path as it runs between the park road on your right and the

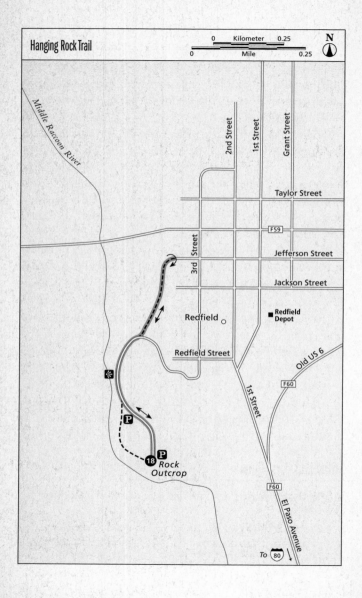

river on your left. Walking along the path, you'll see a space in the trees on your left that leads to a river overlook.

0.3 The path splits—follow the left fork as it moves away from the park road.

0.5 Arrive at the path's end at a residential neighborhood. Turn around and retrace your steps back to the trailhead. (Option: It's just a block from here to the Raccoon River Valley Trail, where you veer right onto the path and walk a couple of blocks to an old depot.)

1.0 Arrive back at the rock outcrop and trailhead.

19 Raccoon River Valley Trail

Redfield, a farming town 30 miles west of Des Moines, is home to this stretch of the 56-mile Raccoon River Valley Trail, which runs west-northwest from the outskirts of Des Moines into wide open farm country. The hike actually doesn't go by the river, but it has some nice views, and if you keep going about 9 miles, you come to the historic courthouse town of Adel.

Distance: 2.0 miles out and back
Approximate hiking time: 1 hour
Difficulty: Easy (flat, smooth surface)
Trail surface: Paved path
Best seasons: Spring through fall
Other trail users: Cyclists, snowmobilers
Canine compatibility: Leashed dogs permitted
Fees and permits: Daily permit required. Payment envelopes are available at the trailhead.

Schedule: 8 a.m. to 10 p.m. daily
Map: USGS Redfield
Trail contacts: Dallas County Conservation Board, 14581 K Ave., Perry 50220; (515) 465-3577; www.conservation.co .dallas.ia.us. Raccoon River Valley Trail Association, 402 Main Street, Suite 1, Cooper 50059; (515) 386-5488; http:// raccoonrivervalleytrail.org
Other: Restroom and historical displays available in the depot building at the trailhead

Finding the trailhead: Drive west from Des Moines on I-80. Take exit 100 (Eldorado Avenue/Dallas CR F60) and drive north 5 miles, crossing over the South Raccoon River on the way (the road becomes El Paso Avenue), to the town limits of Redfield. Follow the road as it forks to the left (First Street), then take the next fork to the right (CR P46/First Street). Look for the old depot, which is set back a little on the right side of the road, across the street from a large grain elevator and farmers' co-op. Park in the depot's adjoining gravel parking lot, alongside the trail. Payment envelopes for trail permits are in a container in front of the depot. GPS: N41 35.263' / W94 11.737'

The Hike

Starting out at Redfield's modest old train depot, you begin by skirting the town, with the path going by some old farmhouses. Soon enough, you see the cornfields—they loom up on your right, as the path enters a section where it's lined on both sides by trees. Cyclists whiz by, taking advantage of the long, straight stretches between towns on this path.

The trail runs parallel to the highway as it leaves town, but there's still plenty of foliage: black-eyed Susans and anemone are just some of the flowers you may spot along the edge of the path and farther back among the trees as you walk.

The path continues past a few houses after you've left Redfield. Near one of them is an impressive collection of birdhouses. Soon after, cross over a creek; the path really opens up as it exits the tree cover.

Walk past a large brick factory on your left and then reach a bridge before turning around and heading back to the depot. Take a moment to survey the land: There is nothing but wide open space as far as the eye can see.

When you make it back to the depot, check out some of the historical photographs inside. There's more history here as well: A nearby farm served as a stop on the Underground Railroad used by slaves fleeing north, just one of several such stops in Iowa.

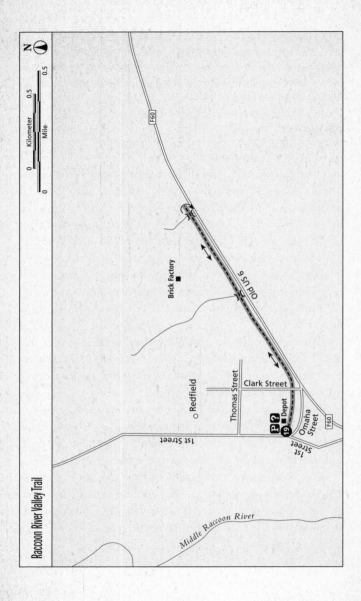

Raccoon River Valley Trail

N

Kilometer   0   0.5
Mile   0   0.5

F60

Brick Factory

Old US 6

Redfield

Thomas Street

Clark Street

1st Street

1st Street

Omaha Street

Depot

P ?

19

F60

Middle Raccoon River

Miles and Directions

0.0 Facing toward the depot and away from the road, walk along the path with the depot on your left. A small creekbed soon comes into view on your right.

0.2 Cross Clark Street at the intersection with Omaha Street. Continue walking on the paved path.

0.6 Cross a bridge over a creek. Walk past a brick factory on your left, then cross over a driveway.

1.0 Reach a bridge over a creek. Turn around and head back to the depot.

2.0 Arrive back at the depot and trailhead.

Clubs and Trail Groups

In addition to the websites mentioned in the trail listings for county conservation boards, the following groups and sites offer good information on hiking in Des Moines and central Iowa.

Des Moines Bicycle Collective
617 Grand Ave.
Des Moines 50309
(515) 288-8022
www.dsmbikecollective.org
Focused more on cycling, this organization also publishes an excellent map of Des Moines area trails that is worth picking up before you head out on a hike.

Iowa Natural Heritage Foundation
505 Fifth Ave., Suite 444
Des Moines 50309-2321
(515) 288-1846
www.inhf.org
This statewide, nonprofit group helps protect and restore natural habitats, including establishing trails. Click on the "Iowa by Trail" button to look for specific trails.

www.greaterdesmoinestrails.org
This clearinghouse of information on trails in and around Des Moines includes maps, trail condition updates, and links to other trail-related groups.

www.mycountyparks.com
This searchable site covers all county parks in Iowa. The site allows you to look up a list of all parks in any county in the state, and also includes an interactive map that allows you to find details on each park, including information on hiking and other activities. The site also has an extensive, up-to-date calendar of events.

www.traillink.com or www.railstotrails.org
These sites offer searchable lists of hikes nationwide, including in Iowa.

About the Author

Michael Ream has been an avid hiker since his parents first took him onto trails in California at age two. He earned a master's degree in journalism from the Medill School of Journalism at Northwestern University and has written for publications including *Midwest Traveler, Southern Traveler,* and *Saveur,* as well as penning several guidebooks. He met his wife on a hiking trip and first brought his daughter hiking when he carried her down the trail on his back. He lives in Des Moines, Iowa, with his family.

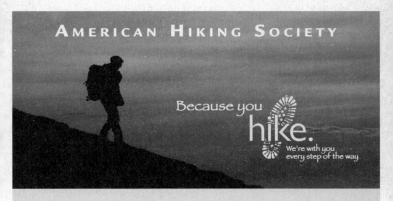